2 GRRRLS

Hello Gorgeous

A Guide to Style

By Kristen Kemp

Scholastic Inc.
New York Toronto London Auckland Sydney
Mexico City New Delhi Hong Kong

ISBN 0-439-18737-0

Copyright © 2000 by 2 GRRRLS, Inc.

Cover and interior design by Louise Bova

Published by Scholastic Inc. All rights reserved.

12 11 10 9 8 7 6 5 4 3 2 1   0 1 2 3 4 5/0

Printed in the U.S.A.
First Scholastic printing, October 2000

Table of Contents

HELLO GORGEOUS!
You Gotta Read This!

*H*i, hello, how are you? So, you wanna know all about style? You've come to the perfect place to get the fashion 411. This book will tell you all you need to know about being gorgeous — inside and out! The thing is, every girl has her own style — it's part of what makes her who she is. Style isn't just about clothes. No way! Style is much more. It's the way you act, what you say, what you think, and what you like.

Whether you are a girlie girl, a groovy girl, a go-for-it girl, or a glamour girl, what's most important is who you are on the inside. Inner style is the coolest thing around, and it isn't something you can buy. Girls with inner style have a way of thinking and feeling good about themselves. And they know what they like. So they each have their own personal style of clothes that feel cool and comfortable to them.

Style is about feeling fab from top to bottom. It's fun to feel and look your very best. This book will help you find a style that's totally you. Just think . . . are you more of a girlie, groovy, go-for-it, or glamour girl? You can read about these different kinds of girls and figure out if you connect with one of their styles. Do you like to wear ignore-me-if-you-can colors or more stunningly simple clothes? When you start to answer these questions, you'll learn all about your own personal style!

So get reading and you'll start to uncover your own style secrets. The bottom line is easy: Style is about celebrating your own special beauty. You've got it, girl. Now express it! Be the girl you wanna be!

be the girl you wanna be be the girl you wanna be

Chapter 1

Girlie Girls: Discover Your Inner Princess!

Are you a girlie girl? Read on and see!

Girlie Girls on the Inside

So what's so special about a girlie girl? Well, a girlie girl just loves being a girl. It's so much fun! Not only does a girlie girl love to dress up for parties, but she loves all the frills in life — like presents wrapped with big bows, pillowcases with ruffles, and smelling flowers in the spring. These kinds of things make a girlie girl smile.

You've heard of sugar and spice and everything nice, right? Well, that is exactly what a girlie girl is all about. She's supersweet. She's kind to her friends and always tries to let them know how important they are to her. But she's nice to everyone, really, and she makes it a point to never say anything mean that might hurt someone's feelings. Sometimes, a girlie girl can be a little shy when meeting new people, but she likes everyone she meets.

A girlie girl always thinks about the people around her. She does whatever she can to make them feel happy. She'll share her candy and genuinely give out compliments — it makes her feel good to help other people feel good, too.

A girlie girl is very organized. She keeps her room neat and tidy, and her closet is in perfect order. There is zero clutter at the bottom of her locker. She's totally together.

And oh so important: A girlie girl believes in true love. She's strong enough and sweet enough to write her own fairy tales. And she believes that one day they could come true.

HELLO PRINCESS!
A Girlie Girl's Sweet Style

A girlie girl's as sweet on the outside as she is on the inside. Are you a girlie girl? Do you love pretty things? A girlie girl always wants to wear nice outfits — even if she's going to a baseball game she'd rather wear a sundress with her sneakers than cutoff jean shorts. And if her dress ties in a big bow in the back, all the better! A girlie girl loves to look that nice.

A girlie girl is the queen of coordinating things. She wants everything to match — even her backpack and her ponytail ribbons. She is known for having the same flowery, pretty prints on the top of her outfits as on the bottom. Sometimes her shirt has the same border as her pants — she likes things to look like they go together. A girlie girl loves to wear clothes made from fluttery materials in pretty pastel colors with little cute earrings. And oh, my! A girlie girl never ever forgets to accessorize — she loves matching bracelets made from beads, buttons, and beautiful shiny jewels.

And a girlie girl is notoriously neat. A girlie girl doesn't deal well with wrinkles or old holey shoes — she wants to look good! Just like she wants her room to always be spotless and clean, she wants her clothes to be pressed and perfect.

Girlie Girl

MEET RELLA —
She's a Girlie Girl

*R*ella is the kind of girl who tries really hard to make everything perfect. She can't stand it when people are sad or upset, so she always goes out of her way to make sure her friends are happy. Doing things for them — and for her family — makes her feel very special inside.

But because she likes everything to be perfect, Rella sometimes worries a lot. That's the drawback of being a perfectionist, you know.

Like a lot of girlie girls, Rella is superorganized — even about what she eats. She likes to give everyone advice about the food pyramid. She constantly reminds her friends that they need at least five servings of fruits and vegetables each and every day. She's just worried about her friends and family being as healthy as possible. Sometimes she cooks for them to make sure they are eating well. Rella even bakes special treats for her kitty, Iris. She loves her fat white cat.

Rella loves feminine outfits with flower patterns or lacy trim. She has more skirts and dresses than anything else in her closet. Wearing pink is practically a Rella requirement — even her sneakers are pretty in pink. She says the perfect outfits make her feel like a princess!

"I really want to design clothes. I can't think of anything better than making a dress that makes someone feel perfect when she puts it on. I know that feeling pretty starts on the inside, but it's nice to have clothes that make you feel special, too."

Girlie Girl

11

A Perfect Fit! Fun Rella Facts

With her love for perfectly pretty clothes, it's no surprise that Rella dreams of being a fashion design diva one day! It's a great job for someone who is so into details — because sewing and designing take a lot of care and thought. Rella dreams of one day putting together fancy fabrics with sweet, beautiful patterns to make fabulously girlie-girl gowns.

Girlie Girl

The Girlie Girl Look

Rella's Tips

1. Look for skirts, skirts, and more skirts. They go over great for any occasion and always make you look feminine — and feel even sweeter, too!

2. Really cute, matching shoes can make an outfit — so pick them carefully. For example, you'll want to wear loafers with casual outfits, dress-up shoes with skirts. Make sure they look great before hitting the pavement. And even more important, try your shoes on at home first! You don't want your toes to hurt when you hit the street!

3. Always iron your clothes. You can't have creases and unruly wrinkles. "Well, not if you're into being neat like me." So ask a pro — like Mom or Dad —to give you the basics. Then wrangle those wrinkles until they're superstraight.

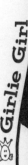

Girlie Girl

4. Accessories that match your shirts or skirts make your clothes look really cute! The right colored earrings or bracelets are Rella essentials. She has a dragonfly necklace to go with her purple dragonfly T-shirt. As she says, the grand rule of being girlie is to accessorize, accessorize, accessorize!

5. So it's no surprise that a fabulous purse is a very important thing to have! "You need a place to put your tissues for when you cry in movies."

6. Rings are king, too! Plastic, metal, cheap, or borrowed — as long as they're colorful, they're number one!

7. If you need to uplift an outfit — just add some matching barrettes for a fast fix!

What Rella Has to Say About Inner Style

"Do sweet things for other people! That will make you feel really, really, really great!"

"I really like to be organized and prepared. I'm a neat person, so I like my clothes to be tidy, too!"

"Things I wear don't mean as much to me as my friends do. I'd give away every piece of clothing I have before I'd ever give up Looie and Roxy and Tutti. I just hope they'll lend me something so I won't be naked!"

Her Fashion Motto!

"Everyone should feel free to think pink – it's cute and delicate and makes you feel like a princess!"

15

Chapter 2

Groovy Girls: Get Real and Get Down!

Are you upbeat and up on the trends?
Maybe you're a groovy girl. . . .

Groovy Girls on the Inside

A groovy girl is ultra-cool. She's in the groove. She's one of the hippest girls around. A groovy girl knows all about what's steaming hot right now and what's just around the bend as far as trends go. She makes it her job to know what's going on. Whether it's the next groovin' dance move or the best new book, a groovy girl is in the know.

A groovy girl is also a great bud. She's the best for giving good advice. And if laughter is the best medicine, a groovy girl can cure you of whatever is wrong. A groovy girl is full of jokes and fun.

Part of the reason a groovy girl is so much fun to be around is because she is super-confident. She believes in herself, and she believes in her friends. She is the best whenever you need a boost. She makes her friends feel extra good by telling them, "You go, girl!" She knows you can be anything you want to be, and she encourages her friends to feel the same way.

A groovy girl never misses a beat.

Absolutely Fabulous! A Groovy Girl's Superchic Style

A groovy girl is as "in style" as can be. She wears the ultimate outfits that are the peak of fashion. She always has a clue as to what the new look will be. If it's gotta-have-it gear, a groovy girl's already got it. If something was popular last year, you can bet that a groovy girl won't want to wear it this year. She can't help it — she just loves to be up-to-the-second with trends and fashions. To make sure her look is fresh and up-to-date, a groovy girl gets her clothing cues from magazines and TV. She'll flip through the pages or channels to see what's popular and what looks good. After all, a groovy girl isn't into fads that aren't flattering. Even though she's hip, she doesn't want to wear something that looks silly just because it's in style. For a groovy girl, being in vogue means looking and feeling good — not just trying to look like everyone else. A groovy girl also hits the mall and checks out all the shops. She'll spend tons of time looking in nice stores — and trying on everything in sight. But she tries to buy stuff on sale. It can be expensive keeping up with the latest clothing crazes.

One thing a groovy girl adores is wearing dark colors — especially black — because it is sophisticated and makes a statement. But since a groovy girl has a brilliant and colorful personality, she likes to add splashes of purple and red and orange and baby blue (or what-ever the "in" color is) to her funky, cool outfits.

So see, it's a done deal — a groovy girl is a certified style queen! But she's also a queen of being positive and confident and inspiring her friends — and that's what makes her so fabulous!

MEET ROXY —
She's a Groovy Girl

*W*hen Roxy's around, there are sure to be loads of laughs. That's because she's just about the funniest girl in her whole town. She is very positive and loves to make people smile. And forget about being shy! Roxy doesn't have a reserved nerve in her entire body — she's superfriendly and outgoing.

Roxy has an I-can-do-it attitude — both mentally and physically. Like when she started swimming last summer, she loved the sport so much that she decided to try to get really good. She swam almost every day, and she figures she must have made it all the way to the state of Iowa — in laps, that is. Now she's even on the swim team. She tackles everything in life with tons of energy and a really positive frame of mind.

Roxy's real love is singing — she's way into music. She sings all of the time because it makes her happy. She's in tune with the music scene and can belt out all the hits. And she always knows who the next big band will be. And her groovin' moves really light up the dance floor. Of course, she teaches all the steps to her buds so they can all get down together.

When it comes to fashion, Roxy dresses in full force. She always looks up-to-date and oh-so-stylish in everything she wears. She loves black outfits because they are really sleek, but she also knows that you can dress up your favorite jeans with a red velvety top. She has a lot of looks, but they are all modern and trendy.

"I can't think of a better job for me! I'd love to be on TV and share my jokes with everyone. I love the idea of making lots of people laugh. Then I could play some cool videos, because good music puts everyone in a great mood. Feeling good is important. Being happy helps me get through anything that comes my way. And I think the fact that I'm happy on the inside makes me a stronger person on the outside."

Groovy Girl

21

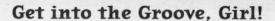

Get into the Groove, Girl!

Because Roxy loves music, she wants to be a VJ when she's older. And to Roxy, the only thing better than sharing music is making people laugh — so if she's a VJ she can do both.

Looking Groovy and Great!

Roxy's Take

1. When in doubt, wear black. It's instantly stylish and, well, chic!

2. But always add a little color somewhere! A red purse, pink scarf, or purple jacket adds life to basic black. "You could even just change your plain old white shoelaces! I love the ones that are fluorescent pink!"

3. A cool pair of shoes can really update your look. Since you wear shoes with so many outfits, you should feel really good about them.

Groovy Girl

4. "Definitely try this if you want to feel fab!" This is something that'll make you look great in anything: Put an outfit on and crank up the tunes. You'll have a happy, I-look-great attitude if you boogie in your outfit first in your bedroom.

5. Fashion mags send lots of messages — some good, some bad. Only pick out the trends that you think will make you look and feel good — the ones that make you feel most like yourself.

6. Always ask people you trust for their fashion advice. They can give you great ideas and tips you never even dreamed of!

What Roxy Has to Say About Inner Style

"I try to be totally open-minded all of the time. I don't like people to judge me, and I don't like to judge other people. Besides, being open-minded makes you a better person. And if you're open-minded, you'll have much more fun trying new things and new styles, too!"

"Sharing your sense of humor makes you beautiful inside and out. So go ahead and wear the best accessory – a smile!"

Her Fashion Motto!

"I love to wear the latest styles and a great big smile – they both help me look and feel my very best!"

Chapter 3

Go-for-It Girls: Learn to Walk on Your Wild Side!

Do you have what it takes to be a go-for-it girl?

Go-for-It Girls on the Inside

Watch out when a go-for-it girl is on the loose! A go-for-it girl is totally up-tempo. She has to be. She has a ton of interests and hobbies and is always racing to get everything done. She's constantly on the move! A go-for-it girl is supersporty and very sure of herself — she's a tomgirl in every way. Some people might say she's a little wild. That's because she's not afraid to take risks and she's not afraid to have fun.

A go-for-it girl is gutsy — she sticks up for what she believes in. She has a gut feeling for what is right and wrong, and she always stands up for what she believes is right. She won't take any baloney from bullies, especially if they are picking on one of her buds. She'll stand by her friends until the end.

The other thing about a go-for-it girl is that she is independent. She likes to do a lot of things on her own. She loves to discover things by herself and make up her own mind. She keeps herself busy and doesn't need a lot of friends, but she is superloyal to the ones that she does have.

You Go Girl

Comfortably Casual! A Go-for-It Girl's Laid-back Style

It wouldn't suit a go-for-it girl to be fussy about fashion — or about anything else, for that matter. Her clothes have to be practical because you can bet that she is on the move. She likes them to be extra comfy. A go-for-it girl wears clothes that make her feel confident. She likes basic jeans, bright colors, and funky T-shirt logos. You can tell she's an athlete — she wears a lot of racing stripes and running shoes. When she's on the court or the field, she opts for sweats and athletic tank tops. And she likes to wear her hair in wash-and-go styles — either supershort so she doesn't have to blow-dry it or a little longer so she can pull it into a ponytail as she's running out the door.

A go-for-it girl isn't into dressing up. Her parents have to talk her into wearing nice clothes. Don't even think she'll put on a dress — not if she doesn't have to, anyway.

There's one thing that's almost always the same for a go-for-it girl — her shoe selection. A go-for-it girl lives in her sneakers and comfy hiking boots.

She doesn't work too hard to keep up with the hottest looks. It doesn't really matter to her what anyone else thinks — to her, being in style means that she's wearing what she's comfortable in. She stays true to herself both in how she acts and how she looks.

MEET LOOIE —
She's a Go-for-It Girl

*L*ooie's a total tomgirl, and nothing holds her back. She knows that if she goes for her dreams, they'll come true. That's why she's always on the go — she's got a lot of dreams to make reality!

One of her dreams is to be really great at sports. She especially loves soccer and can beat any of the boys, but she's totally into her all-girls team. Being ultra-athletic, she feels prepared for any challenge.

And she's sure to challenge anyone who picks on one of her friends. She's willing to fight for what she feels is right. The thing about Looie is, even though she's brave enough to stand up to bullies, she's also a little bit shy. It takes a long time to get to know her because she is so independent. She's not good at small talk or chatting in the locker room. But she has no problem talking with her close friends because she feels so comfortable with them.

She loves spending time with her buds, but she also likes to have time alone to read books, work on her Web site, or watch TV. She can do a million things at once!

When it comes to her wardrobe, Looie's top priority is comfort. She needs clothes that won't hold her back. It's all about jeans, leggings, sweats, fleece, and flannel for her. When she wants to dress up (well, she never wants to dress up), she might put on a colorful cotton waffle top and her favorite pair of capri pants. Whatever she wears, she's always ready for a pickup basketball game or a hike in the park.

On the Go! Looie's Got It Together!

Looie is supersmart, and she loves to figure things out. Maybe that's why she's so good at working with computers. She's always using the latest gadgets for her Web creations. That's probably what she'll do one day — design Web pages about important causes. Or maybe she'll be a doctor who researches devastating diseases. She's really not sure. There are so many options! She does know that she wants to make a difference. And she knows if she works really hard to follow her dreams, she can make them come true!

> "The thing that makes me happiest is just being myself. I love being an athlete, being smart at school, and helping my friends with their homework. I know I can be gutsy, but I'm also kind of shy — if that makes any sense. I am all kinds of things all rolled into one. I am just me! And I never try to be anything else."

A Real Princess

believes in love and fairy tales

Rella

Gorgeous Girl

beauty comes from within

Tutti

A Go-for-It Girl's Dress Code

Looie's Advice

1. Try jeans that have stretchy stuff in them. Also, look for wide-leg pants. They not only look hip, they also adjust to unplanned games of tag or kickball.

2. Skirts AREN'T for everyone and that's okay!

3. Whenever you need a boost, just wear your favorite color. Looie likes to wear red. It's bright and full of energy — just like a go-for-it girl.

4. Looie borrows a lot of clothes from her brothers. She loves their longer shorts and thicker socks. "I really think those striped socks last longer!"

Go-For-It-Girl

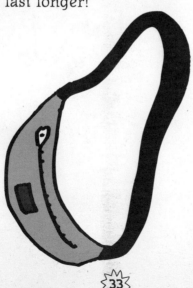

5. Wearing a colorful cotton crew tee to school makes getting set for soccer practice a cinch! She only has to change her jeans to shorts, and she's ready to play ball!

6. Skiwear doubles for really cool winter clothes. Looie especially loves down coats and vests.

7. Sticking to styles that are versatile is much more important than staying totally in fashion. That's true for Looie, at least.

8. "And you can't forget — cotton is the comfiest fabric ever."

What Looie Has to Say About Inner Style

"Being active and athletic makes me feel good about myself. And when I feel fit, I feel fantastic. So it always reminds me of my strengths!"

"I'm not afraid to speak up. I like to wear clothes that can speak up, too! I think people get the idea that I don't care what anybody thinks – but in a good way!"

"My inner style is about being the best all-around person that I can be. That means trying hard at everything I do."

Her Fashion Motto!

"Make sure your colorful clothes can keep up with everything you do!"

Chapter 4

Glamour Girls: Get in Touch with Your Inner Superstar!

Are you a natural entertainer, a born superstar?
Maybe you're a glamour girl. . . .

Glamour Girls on the Inside

A glamour girl has her very own style — she's a real original. Nobody sees things quite like a glamour girl. She's very dramatic and vibrant. When she's happy, she wears the biggest smile and always laughs really loud, but she also gets supersad sometimes. Some people might say she's moody, but it's just that she's very passionate about everything and everyone. She really lets her emotions show.

A glamour girl glows with energy and individuality. She knows that beauty comes from within, and she casts a spell on almost everyone with her genuine charm. She also appreciates the inner beauty of her buds. She loves to really get to know a person — right down to their quirkiest detail.

Sometimes, though, a glamour girl can be a little bossy. She has such great ideas for things to do that she can be a little too enthusiastic and might overwhelm her friends. She can also be supersensitive and take things too personally, but she always picks herself up again.

Above all, a glamour girl is a true entertainer. When she tells her amazing stories, everyone turns to listen. Sure, she might exaggerate sometimes, but no one can resist her tall tales.

Glamour Girl

You Look Marvelous: Glamour Girls Shine Like a Star!

Glamour isn't just about wearing fancy clothes — it's a feeling that comes from deep inside of you. A glamour girl has something special that always makes her sparkle. Whether she's wearing a shiny silver T-shirt, a bright red dress, or a funky-patterned hippie shirt with bell-bottom jeans, you can bet a glamour girl looks and feels like a star. She has so much inner beauty, she's almost electric!

A glamour girl isn't all that interested in keeping up with the latest look. She has a look that's all her own. Her clothes are a little over-the-top — just like her personality. It's hard to walk into a room and not notice a glamour girl.

You won't find a glamour girl doing all her shopping at a department store or even through catalogs. She likes things that not everyone else will have. She'll wear checked miniskirts, purple velvet pants, or a lime-green sweater vest. She loves wearing hats, shiny jewelry, and all kinds of belts. That's why she's serious about secondhand stores. She spends a lot of time in search of the perfect retro threads. (You know, retro means stuff that was popular years ago and still looks supercool today.) A glamour girl also checks out her mom's closet for finds. She thinks it's fun to wear clothes that her mom wore when she was her age. A glamour girl loves the way fancy old clothes make her feel — like someone with her own sense of style, like a movie star!

Glamour Girl

MEET TUTTI —
She's a Glamour Girl

*O*ne look at Tutti and you'll understand — she's a glamour girl through and through. People have been known to give her a stare or two, because she's got that special something. Tutti's beauty comes from within. She's sweet and charming and energetic. She's a complete original, and she loves to learn about all the things that make other people ultra-unique as well.

Tutti can be emotional and sensitive, but that's what will make her such a great actress one day, which is definitely what she wants to be. She's very intense — when Tutti is happy, everyone can tell. And when she's upset, she's not afraid to cry a little, too. She doesn't like to keep her feelings a secret — she prefers to let them loose.

Tutti's a devoted member of the local drama club. She's played all sorts of parts, from a giraffe to an Egyptian princess, and she almost always gets a standing ovation. Tutti is talented, in case you couldn't tell!

When she's getting dressed, Tutti treats every outfit like a costume. One day she might wear a button-down shirt with one of her brother's neckties. And the next day she'll sport her plaid kilt with a matching beret. She just loves the cute 1960s dresses, hats, and gloves that her aunts give to her. Her mother's hippie getups are lots of fun, too. She also has a great beaded hat that looks like it's from the flapper era. But her prized possession is a poodle skirt from the fifties.

Tutti wants every outfit she puts on to be dramatic and one-of-a-kind — just like she is. But more important, she tries to be outgoing and vibrant in everything she says and does.

Glamour Girl

Let Tutti Entertain You!

Tutti was bitten by the acting bug at a very early age. It started when she was six and went to New York City for a family vacation. She climbed to the top of the Statue of Liberty, and when she saw the big buildings and all of the people, her imagination went wild. She decided she was meant to move to the Big Apple one day and be on Broadway!

And it helps that she can even cry on cue!

"I don't tell many people how I can make myself cry because that would give away my secret. But I always think of how sad I would be without my dog, Elroy. He is so special, and I'd be so upset if anything happened to him. If that doesn't bring on the tears, I have to pinch myself really hard. But that's only in emergencies!"

Who Doesn't Want to Hear Someone Say, "Hello, Gorgeous?"

Tutti's Clues to Capturing the Glamour Girl Glow

1. One special accessory or piece of clothing can make a normal outfit look more spectacular. Look for a cheap pair of big-rimmed glasses (without a prescription) or a sparkly fake diamond headband to add some style.

2. When going for the hippie look, try to find shirts with flowers and tapered sleeves that get wider around your wrists. They are supercheap at secondhand stores.

3. Simple hair accessories are a must. For a neat and tailored look, try clipping a baby barrette just below your bangs. For a fifties flair, tie a rolled-up scarf around a ponytail.

4. From top to bottom, an outfit must be completely "put together." You should try it on and make sure it's perfect before you hit the town (or school!).

5. "Retro bags and purses are much cuter than anything new!" Check out the local thrift stores for any kind of handbag — from sequins to plastic. They all look super-cute!

6. If you don't feel glamorous, add a cute cardigan sweater to your outfit.

7. Mix and match whatever you want. "I like to put funky colors together — even if they don't exactly match. As long as it looks good to me, I feel good wearing it."

What Tutti Has to Say About Inner Style

"Sometimes people just don't get my look. I like it, though, so I wear my clothes with pride. I have found out that people actually admire me for not being afraid to be unique!"

"I am a great listener! Doing small things for other people makes me feel really good inside."

"Caring about clothes is cool – but caring about other important things is even cooler. Always ask other people what's up in their lives. And show a lot of friendliness and concern for people, even if you don't know them that well."

Her Fashion Motto!

"If you want to really shine, invent your own style. Be brave and be yourself!"

Chapter 5

Quiz-o-rama! What Is Your Own Super Style?

QUIZ 1: WHAT'S YOUR INNER STYLE?

Take this quiz to find out your inner style. Just check each statement that is true for you!

 _____ You love to talk to other people to find out what's important to them. You're into discovering everyone's endearing quirks.

 _____ You are really good at sports or school or something else. And you admit it, your awesome abilities make you feel great about yourself.

 _____ Say you're at the movies and your friend is down in the dumps. You'd find it impossible to pay attention to the flick because you'd be so worried about her.

 _____ People tell you that you're the most positive person they know.

 _____ You're known for being a completely unique girl.

 _____ Being helpful and caring for other people is just a part of your personality! You love to take care of others.

 _____ When a bug is on the loose and everyone else is squealing, you are always the one who is brave enough to pick it up.

 _____ You're expressive and emotional – you can cry or be happy at the drop of a hat.

 _____ Making others smile and laugh just comes naturally to you.

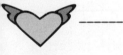 _____ People tell you that you have an amazing ability to do a bunch of things at once. You have a ton of hobbies.

 _____ You love being the center of attention. When you tell a story at the lunch table, everyone's all ears.

 _____ Your friends sometimes tease you (in a nice way!) for being so neat and orderly.

 _____ Reading is a fun way to get lost in your favorite fantasies. You love to have some time alone.

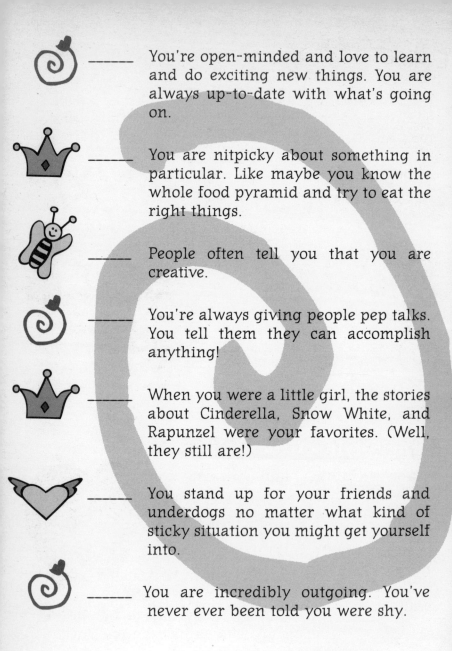

_____ You're open-minded and love to learn and do exciting new things. You are always up-to-date with what's going on.

_____ You are nitpicky about something in particular. Like maybe you know the whole food pyramid and try to eat the right things.

_____ People often tell you that you are creative.

_____ You're always giving people pep talks. You tell them they can accomplish anything!

_____ When you were a little girl, the stories about Cinderella, Snow White, and Rapunzel were your favorites. (Well, they still are!)

_____ You stand up for your friends and underdogs no matter what kind of sticky situation you might get yourself into.

_____ You are incredibly outgoing. You've never ever been told you were shy.

SCORING:

Count up how many times you checked each design. Find the design you marked the most and read the description below.

MOSTLY 👑 :

Inner style = Girlie Girl

Your personal style is to be calm and caring, neat and sweet. You are super-organized, so you always have time to do something nice for your buds. You'd do absolutely anything for other people. You want nothing more than to make them happy! You love fairy tales and you believe in true love! These things make you a sweet and beautiful person inside and out.

MOSTLY 🌀 :

Inner style = Groovy Girl

You're funnier and happier than anybody in three bordering states. You don't want to dwell on unhappy thoughts when there are so many beautiful things to think about instead. You stay totally open to just about every-thing at all times. That makes you an understanding and trustworthy friend.

Mostly 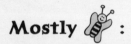:

Inner style = Go-for-It Girl

You're not afraid of bullies or bugs, and a lot of people wish they had nerves of steel like you! You are also a high-energy person who can whiz through a thousand things before noon. Plus you are always on the move and won't let things hold you back. And your awesome abilities — sports, school, or something else — make you feel confident about yourself.

Mostly :

Inner style = Glamour Girl

Creative and kind and really unique — that's totally you! You aren't afraid of what other people think. Instead, you'll go out on a limb and do things that make you feel fabulous and glamorous. You are very emotional, though — you can't help it if you feel everything very deeply. Because of that trait, you might make a great drama diva one day! If not, you will always entertain your friends with your far-out tales.

QUIZ 2: WHAT'S YOUR FASHION FORTE?

Find out which brand of style has the same fashion cues as you! Just check each statement that is true for you!

_____ You try to wear outfits that are totally you, that no one else would wear.

_____ You like wearing black. It's sleek and chic and easy to match!

_____ You think pink a lot. You also love purple and pastels.

_____ You avoid skirts at all costs! You don't dress up unless you have to.

_____ Sometimes you watch TV just to check out the clothes.

_____ You like secondhand stores more than the mall.

_____ You like clothes that are as casual as you are.

_____ You always coordinate your clothes from head to toe.

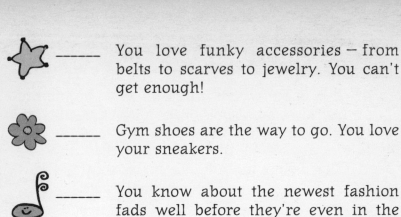 _____ You love funky accessories — from belts to scarves to jewelry. You can't get enough!

_____ Gym shoes are the way to go. You love your sneakers.

_____ You know about the newest fashion fads well before they're even in the stores.

_____ People sometimes tell you that you can carry off any kind of clothes because you have a unique sense of style.

_____ You like dresses with beads and bows, and jewels and rings are very good things.

_____ You will wear anything that you feel comfortable in.

_____ Your friends sometimes tell you they wish they could be as sophisticated as you.

_____ You don't like to look wrinkled. You are too neat for that! You also like your shoes to be clean.

SCORING:

:

It's the same drill as Quiz 1. Count up how many times you checked each design. Find the design you marked the most and read the description below to find your fashion fit!

Girlie Girl

Patterns and prints and perfectly matched outfits — that's you. If something is feminine and soft and fluttery, you want to wear it. You feel your best wearing dresses and neatly coordinated shirts and skirts. You probably love to think pink! Your style is girlie through and through!

Groovy Girl

You go for modern clothes in the chicest styles and colors. You've always gotten your favorite fashion ideas from TV and mags. And that's totally cool — you love the way it feels to wear the latest looks. But the best part is that you manage to always look completely sophisticated, even if you're wearing jeans and a tee. You have a magical way of making today's trends work.

Go-for-It Girl

Yes, you like your sportswear, and that's because comfort and function are key when it comes to your clothing. You can't stand outfits that keep you from doing things. Your clothes need to move around as much as you do! If you want to play a game of kick-the-can or hang out on the jungle gym, you don't want your clothes to get in the way. And you would never wear a skirt if you didn't have to — no way!

Glamour Girl

Not only do you like your clothes to grab attention, you like them to be glamorous and gorgeous, too. You don't look to the latest trends to find your style. You'd rather find duds that say something about you — and sometimes they're pieces from the past. You like colorful hats or funky sunglasses that stand out a little. You're so confident, you can pull it off. And you look great in anything you wear.

Are You Quiz Confused?

Say you took both quizzes and you ended up with a different inner and outer style. Don't worry. It just means you're an individual. Yay! And that's what we're really trying to tell you here.

If you found out that you have a groovy personality but like to wear girlie and glamorous clothes, that's cool. You just need to know that you should wear what you like and act the way that makes you comfortable. That's what is so important. So you can be the girl you wanna be.

Chapter 6

Get-Gorgeous Tricks from the Grrrls

Rella and Roxy and Looie and Tutti have all found their own styles, and they have some hints to share. They may not know everything about style, fashion, clothes, and coolness, but they have learned an awful lot! Here are some hot shoppin' secrets. Don't dress without these tips from the Grrrls!

Girls are shoppin'! Here are hints for making the most of your cash stash. See if a few will work for you!

Matching madness

1. Pick a store you really like and hit it often! As much as you can, that is! When you're on the lookout for perfectly paired items, you usually have to get them from the same store — and they can be expensive. So pick out a few matched outfits you like and keep going back until at least one of them is on the sale rack. Then you'll get the cutest clothes cheap!

More matching!

2. Matching clothes can be sooo hard to find. So you can make your own outfits. (Get an adult's help on this project.) You can add sequins, puffy paint, appliqués, or lacy borders that you buy at a fabric store to any T-shirt. Then you can make a matching design around the cuffs of a pair of jeans or the hem of a skirt. An adult can help you with the sewing or using hot glue to apply your designs. In the end, you have a matching outfit that's all you!

No time for shopping?

3. It's true that girls on the go don't have a whole lot of time to shop. The solution? Catalogs! Look for brands you've bought before; that way they're more likely to fit. It's a great way to find cute clothes without using up all of your energy. Some girls would rather play soccer than shop!

Oops! What was it that I wanted to buy?

4. Sometimes when you're out shoppin', you might forget what you went to get! So bring along magazine clippings of the styles you like. That way, you'll be sure to get exactly the right duds! Making a list is always helpful, too.

Don't buy that new look just yet. . . .

5. Never spend too much of your — or your parents' — money on those really trendy items. Buy those in cheaper stores and on sale racks, especially since you won't want to wear them for very long. (Even the coolest style doesn't stay in style forever.) The things that are worth spending more money on are basic clothes like jeans, turtlenecks, sweaters, pants, and skirts.

Happy thrifting!

6. A cheap accessory is always easy to find. Cool coats, shawls, and handbags are a dime a dozen at secondhand stores. And according to a glamour girl, you should never leave home without one!

More thrifting 411 . . .

7. Wanna know where to get retro clothes for cheap? Here are a glamour girl's favorite places:

1) her grandmas' and mother's and aunts' closets (but ask permission first!), 2) small and cute secondhand boutiques, and 3) Salvation Army and Goodwill stores.

Look great for less $$$

8. Go to expensive stores to pick out your look. But don't buy your clothes at the high-priced places. Instead, go to a cheaper store and pick up bargain duds that look just like the costly ones.

Buy this or else — unless you're Looie, that is:

9. Any groovy girl will tell you: Everyone needs a simple, sleek, dark-colored dress.

A new outfit for the price of tights . . .

10. If you want to really jazz up an outfit, buy colored or striped tights. You can have a whole new look and only have to buy a stylish pair of stockings! Striped socks are supercool, too.

Chapter 7

Whatever you Wear, You'll Look Marvelous!

If you're like a lot of girls, you like a lot of styles! You know, you don't have to choose just one. Thank goodness! You can be lots of different styles all rolled into one. Every day you can look a different way.

Didja know?

1. Style swapping

Even a girlie girl wants to look groovy from time to time — like for the school dance. So, the solution is simple: Borrow from a bud. Borrowing clothes is a great option. It's fun to share, especially if you have something your friend wants to wear in return. But always be careful with someone else's clothes!

2. Different moods = different duds

If it's cold outside and you're feeling glum, wear your warmest, coziest sweater. It will instantly give you a boost! Or, if it is one of the first spring days, put on a bright color and let the warm weather soak into your skin.

3. Have to give an oral report?

If you are going to be in front of the entire class giving a speech, it's best to look your best. Looking nice will give you that extra confidence you need and it can lift your spirits, too. It'll make your day!

4. If you wake up in an amazing mood, wear your favorite outfit.

Why? Because it will make your day that much better!

5. Wear what you want.

Just because you're a glamour girl doesn't mean you can't wear athletic gear. Maybe you want to sport standard sweatpants but wear a crazy rhine-stone-studded T-shirt on top. Your sense of style is whatever you want it to be. You can mix and match anything.

How to Get Dressed

No, this isn't about how to put on your clothes. This is about deciding what to wear — there are all sorts of ways. Maybe one of these will work for you:

A GIRLIE GIRL is superorganized and likes to plan everything way ahead. Every night she sets her clothes aside for the next day and has all her ironing done ahead of time.

A GROOVY GIRL goes with the flow. She likes to see how she feels in the morning and picks an outfit that matches her mood.

A GO-FOR-IT GIRL just grabs whatever she can find out of her closet or off her floor. She never really wants to take off her flannel pajamas, so she goes for whatever feels the most comfy.

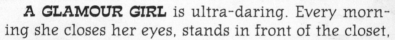

A GLAMOUR GIRL is ultra-daring. Every morning she closes her eyes, stands in front of the closet, and just pulls something out. She never knows if she'll get a skirt or pants or a sweater, but she always finds a way to build an ultra-awesome outfit from whatever she picked.

So, see — you can express yourself with what you wear! Go ahead! Love your life, and wear what you want!

See Ya Later, 'Bye!

Hopefully this book has helped you see that what makes a girl cool is so much more than her clothes, her hair, and her accessories. Those are just small parts of who she is. What she feels inside and how she acts on the outside are so much more important.

When it comes to finding your personal style — inner and outer — it may take more than reading a book to totally figure it out. It takes time to find what works best for you. Your inner girl is cooler than cool. Always give her new chances to come out!

So go, girl. Celebrate something special — celebrate yourself! Be the girl you wanna be™!

Sound Off!

E-mail or write — we wanna know what you think!

For more 2 Grrrls info, just look on our site:
www.2grrrls.com

Address:
2 Grrrls
PO Box 75217
St Paul, MN 55175-0217